# LEA & PERRINS

# EVERYDAY COOKBOOK

## MARILYN HARRISON

D0795278

A MARTIN BOOK

Published by Martin Books,
an imprint of Woodhead-Faulkner Ltd,
Fitzwilliam House, 32 Trumpington Street,
Cambridge CB2 1QY in association with HP Foods Ltd,
Northampton Road, Market Harborough,
Leicestershire LE16 9BG.

First published 1987
© Woodhead-Faulkner Ltd and HP Foods Ltd 1987
ISBN 0 85941 395 0

**British Library Cataloguing in Publication Data**

Harrison, Marilyn
    Lea & Perrins everyday cookbook
    1. Cookery, International
    I. Title
    641.5     TX725.A1
    ISBN 0-85941-395-0

Design: Ken Vail Graphic Design
Photography: Sandy Hedderwick
Food preparation for photography: Marilyn Harrison
Stylist: Nina Barough
Typesetting: Goodfellow & Egan
Printed and bound by Hazell, Watson & Viney Ltd,
Member of the BPCC Group, Aylesbury, Bucks

# INTRODUCTION

John Wheeley Lea and William Perrins founded their business with a chemist's shop which opened in Broad Street, Worcester, in 1823. In addition to the more usual medicines, pills and ointments, chemists in those days used to sell herbs and spices and a variety of imported foods which were not generally available in grocers' shops of the time.

It was probably for this reason that Lord Sandys visited the chemist's shop in 1835 with a recipe for a sauce he had discovered whilst in India. Lord Sandys had held many offices in the East, including that of Governor of Bengal. According to tradition, the sauce when first made was unpalatable, whereupon it was consigned to the Broad Street cellars! A year or so later Messrs. Lea & Perrins were having a clearout and had one last taste before getting rid of it. It was wonderful – it had matured!

Their opinion was echoed by all who tasted it and the fame of Lea & Perrins' Worcestershire Sauce spread across the globe.

Bottles of Worcestershire Sauce have surfaced in some interesting places over the years. In 1903, a Colonel Younghusband paid a pioneering visit to the forbidden Eastern City of Lhasa, only to discover a bottle had found its way there before him! More recently, a bottle was discovered in volcanic rock by archaeologists excavating the buried city of Te Wairoa in New Zealand, which had been overwhelmed by a volcanic eruption in 1886.

The original and genuine Worcestershire Sauce's popularity has continued to spread, and today it is sold in over one hundred countries across the world. The recipe, which consists of entirely natural ingredients matured for up to three years, has been kept a secret since the early days and a flood of imitations has tried, but failed, to replicate the unique taste.

It was in 1906 that the High Court granted Lea & Perrins the sole right to call their Worcestershire Sauce the 'Original and Genuine', two years after the Royal Warrant was granted by Edward VII.

Worcestershire Sauce is so versatile; it is superb with red meat dishes but is also equally good at livening up chicken and fish, and it is not too old-fashioned to work well in microwaved dishes.

1985 saw the 150th Anniversary of Lea & Perrins' Worcestershire Sauce and in 1986 a range of Culinary Sauces was introduced to complement the 'Original and Genuine'.

**Chilli and Garlic** contains wine, sherry and hazelnuts, in addition to chilli and garlic. It is particularly good with red meats, casseroles and bolognese, as it gives a fairly hot and spicy taste with a hint of sweetness.

**Lemon and Herbs** contains orange juice as well as lemon and seven different herbs. It adds a delicate tang to any fish dish and goes well with pork and veal. It also makes an ideal salad dressing when mixed with yoghurt or mayonnaise.

**Spiced Peppercorn** has no fewer than six spices in addition to peppercorns, mustard and onions. It gives a rich, peppery flavour to chicken and steak and it also livens up lasagne or risotto and does a marvellous job of pepping up beefburgers and sausages.

As with Worcestershire Sauce, the only limitation to using Culinary Sauces is the cook's imagination.

**Cookery Notes**
The recipes in this book have been specially created to offer a wide range of dishes, from classics to snacks, entertaining to 'quick and easy'.

Following today's trend of healthier eating, the recipes have been devised to lend themselves easily to a low fat, low salt and high fibre diet. Simply substitute skimmed milk, low fat cheeses, fats and oils high in polyunsaturates and wholemeal products for their corresponding foods in the recipes.

If you have a freezer, there are recipes and ideas just for you. Microwave owners, look out for the microwave hints and tips.

Throughout the book, the symbol ■ denotes suitability for freezing and the symbol ▤ indicates suitability for reheating in a microwave oven.

The recipes give a guide only as to the amount of Lea & Perrins' Worcestershire Sauce and Culinary Sauces to be used – experiment to suit your own tastes and try adapting your own favourite recipes too.

All recipes in the book give ingredients in both metric (g, ml, etc) and imperial (oz, pints, etc). Follow either metric or imperial measures for recipes, but not both. All spoon measures given are level.

# CONVERSION TABLES
*Approximate equivalents*

## OVEN TEMPERATURES

| °C | °F | Gas Mark | Temperature |
|----|-----|----------|-------------|
| 110 | 225 | ¼ | |
| 130 | 250 | ½ | Very cool |
| 140 | 275 | 1 | |
| 150 | 300 | 2 | Cool |
| 170 | 325 | 3 | Warm |
| 180 | 350 | 4 | Moderate |
| 190 | 375 | 5 | |
| 200 | 400 | 6 | Fairly Hot |
| 220 | 425 | 7 | Hot |
| 230 | 450 | 8 | |
| 240 | 475 | 9 | Very Hot |

## WEIGHT

| Imperial | Metric |
|----------|--------|
| 1 oz | 25 g |
| 2 oz | 50 g |
| 3 oz | 75 g |
| 4 oz | 125 g |
| 5 oz | 150 g |
| 6 oz | 175 g |
| 7 oz | 200 g |
| 8 oz | 225 g |
| 9 oz | 250 g |
| 10 oz | 275 g |
| 11 oz | 300 g |
| 12 oz | 350 g |
| 13 oz | 375 g |
| 14 oz | 400 g |
| 15 oz | 425 g |
| 1 lb | 450 g |
| 1½ lb | 700 g |
| 2 lb | 900 g |
| 2½ lb | 1.1 kg |
| 3 lb | 1.4 kg |
| 3½ lb | 1.6 kg |
| 4 lb | 1.8 kg |
| 4½ lb | 2 kg |

## LIQUID CAPACITY

| Imperial | Metric |
|----------|--------|
| 1 fluid oz | 25 ml |
| 2 fluid oz | 50 ml |
| 3 fluid oz | 75 ml |
| 4 fluid oz | 125 ml |
| 5 fluid oz (¼ pint) | 150 ml |
| 6 fluid oz | 175 ml |
| 7 fluid oz | 200 ml |
| 8 fluid oz | 225 ml |
| 9 fluid oz | 250 ml |
| 10 fluid oz (½ pint) | 275 ml |
| 20 fluid oz (1 pint) | 575 ml |
| 35 fluid oz | 1000 ml (1 litre) |

# SAUCES, MARINADES AND DRESSINGS

## SAUCES

A sauce can transform an ordinary, everyday food into something special, by adding different flavours, colours and textures.

## BASIC WHITE SAUCE

*Makes 275 ml (½ pint)*

A very versatile sauce, referred to repeatedly throughout the book, which can be used with many different foods and flavourings.

25 g (1 oz) butter or margarine
25 g (1 oz) flour
275 ml (½ pint) milk
1 tablespoon Worcestershire Sauce *or* 1 tablespoon Lea & Perrins' Lemon and Herbs Sauce *or* 1 tablespoon Lea & Perrins' Chilli and Garlic Sauce *or* 1 tablespoon Lea & Perrins' Spiced Peppercorn Sauce
seasoning, to taste

1 Melt the butter in a saucepan and stir in the flour.
2 Cook gently for a minute, stirring constantly.
3 Remove from heat, add a little milk and blend well.
4 Continue adding the milk gradually until smooth. Return to the heat and bring to the boil, stirring all the time.
5 When the sauce has thickened, remove from the heat and add your chosen flavouring and salt and pepper to taste.

❄ Suitable for freezing.

▤ Reheat from frozen.

# MUSHROOM SAUCE

*Makes 1 litre (1¾ pints)*

Make a quantity of this sauce to keep in the freezer. Serve with grilled meats or liver or serve with pasta and sprinkle with parmesan cheese.

4 tablespoons oil
175 g (6 oz) onions, peeled and sliced
1 clove of garlic, crushed
225 g (8 oz) mushrooms, washed and sliced
575 ml (1 pint) beef stock
2 teaspoons cornflour
2 tablespoons Worcestershire Sauce
213 g (7½ oz) can of tomatoes
2 tablespoons tomato purée
seasoning, to taste

1 Heat the oil in a saucepan, add the onions and garlic and fry gently for about 5 minutes, or until soft and transparent.
2 Stir in the mushrooms and cook gently for 3 minutes.
3 Remove from the heat and pour in the stock, the cornflour blended smoothly with the Worcestershire Sauce, tomatoes, purée and seasoning to taste.
4 Return to the heat and bring to the boil, stirring constantly. Simmer uncovered for 20 minutes, stirring occasionally.

❄ Suitable for freezing.

▤ Reheat from frozen.

# BARBECUE SAUCE

*Makes 425 ml (¾ pint)*

Use to brush on kebabs, spare ribs, beefburgers, sausages or lamb chops during grilling and barbecuing.

4 tablespoons oil
1 large onion, peeled and finely chopped
2 cloves of garlic, crushed
2 tablespoons tomato purée
4 tablespoons soft brown sugar
2 tablespoons wine vinegar
2 tablespoons Lea & Perrins' Chilli & Garlic Sauce
4 teaspoons cornflour
275 ml (½ pint) water
seasoning, to taste

1 Heat the oil in a saucepan and fry the onion and garlic gently for 5 minutes or until the onion is soft.
2 Add the tomato purée, sugar, vinegar and Chilli & Garlic Sauce and stir well.
3 Blend the cornflour to a smooth paste with a little of the water.
4 Remove the saucepan from the heat and stir in the cornflour paste.
5 Return to the heat, cook for 1 minute, stirring constantly then add the remaining water and bring to the boil, still stirring. Season to taste.

▨ Suitable for freezing.

▤ Reheat from frozen.

*Spaghetti with Mushroom Sauce*
*Kebabs brushed with Barbecue Sauce*

*Spare ribs in Honey*
*& Pineapple Marinade*

# SPICY TOMATO SAUCE

*Makes 1.2 litres (2 pints)*

It is very handy to keep a quantity of this sauce in the freezer. Use it in recipes as required or serve it with pasta, beefburgers, meat loaves, etc.

4 tablespoons oil
1 large onion, peeled and chopped
2 cloves of garlic, crushed
1½ kg (3 lb) ripe tomatoes, skinned and chopped *or*
3 × 397 g (14 oz) cans of tomatoes, drained
1 teaspoon sugar
2 tablespoons Worcestershire Sauce
275 ml (½ pint) beef stock
seasoning, to taste

1 Heat the oil in a large saucepan and fry the onion and garlic for 5 minutes or until the onion is transparent.
2 Add the tomatoes and all the remaining ingredients with seasoning to taste.
3 Bring to the boil, stir well, then cover the pan, reduce the heat and allow to simmer gently for 30 minutes, stirring occasionally.
4 Purée the sauce in a blender or food processor.
5 Return it to the saucepan and simmer gently, uncovered for about 20 minutes or until reduced.
6 Taste and adjust seasoning if necessary.

❄ Suitable for freezing.

▤ Reheat from frozen.


# MARINADES

Marinades help to moisten and tenderise meat and poultry, adding flavour and preventing meats from drying out during cooking, especially during barbecuing. Pierce or score the meat to allow the marinade to penetrate and leave it soaking in the marinade for as long as possible – preferably overnight. Simply combine the ingredients in the recipes below and use with sausages, chops, kebabs and spare ribs.

# TOMATO MARINADE

*Makes 125 ml (4 fluid oz)*

1 tablespoon oil
2 tablespoons tomato ketchup
2 tablespoons mustard powder
1 tablespoon Worcestershire Sauce
seasoning, to taste

# HONEY & PINEAPPLE MARINADE

*Makes 275 ml (¹/₂ pint)*

4 tablespoons honey
1¹/₂ teaspoons mustard powder
6 tablespoons lemon juice
3 tablespoons Worcestershire Sauce
3 tablespoons pineapple juice

# HOT CHILLI MARINADE

*Makes 150 ml (¹/₄ pint)*

2 tablespoons oil
2 tablespoons Lea & Perrins' Chilli and Garlic Sauce
2 tablespoons soy sauce
2 tablespoons Worcestershire Sauce
1 tablespoon soft brown sugar
1 tablespoon tomato purée
1 tablespoon wine vinegar
1 teaspoon ground ginger

# DRESSINGS

A good dressing is essential to a salad; use on green salads, and egg, fish, meat and vegetable salads.

## OIL AND VINEGAR DRESSING

*Makes 125 ml (4 fluid oz)*

1 tablespoon Worcestershire Sauce
2 tablespoons white wine vinegar
6 tablespoons olive oil
1 teaspoon French mustard
salt and black pepper

Whisk or shake all the dressing ingredients together, adding chopped fresh herbs if wished.

## FLAVOURED MAYONNAISE DRESSINGS

4 tablespoons mayonnaise
1 tablespoon Worcestershire Sauce *or* 1 tablespoon Lea &
Perrins' Lemon and Herbs Sauce *or* 1 tablespoon Lea & Perrins'
Chilli and Garlic Sauce *or* 1 tablespoon Lea & Perrins' Spiced
Peppercorn Sauce

Blend the ingredients together in a bowl and add chopped fresh herbs if wished. Serve with prawns, tuna, meat, eggs or salads.

*Flavoured Mayonnaise Dressings*
*Cottage cheese dip with Chilli & Garlic Sauce*
*Soured cream dip with spring onions and Lemon & Herbs Sauce*

# DIPS AND SAVOURY BUTTERS

A variety of different flavoured dips can be created quickly and easily using the Lea & Perrins' sauces in the following ways:

Add 1 tablespoon of the Lea & Perrins' sauce of your choice to 5 tablespoons of either mayonnaise, thick plain yogurt, full or low fat soft cheeses, cottage cheese or soured cream.

Add some finely chopped herbs, spring onions, crushed garlic, chopped watercress or grated cheese to make interesting flavours and textures.

Serve individual dips in separate bowls with a selection of raw vegetables, crisps and cheese biscuits for dipping.

Savoury butters are a useful extra to keep in your freezer. They can be used straight from the freezer on grilled meats, poached fish and cooked vegetables. Alternatively, they may be softened for sandwiches, canapés, cheese biscuits and toast.

125 g (4 oz) butter, softened
1 tablespoon Worcestershire Sauce *or*
1 tablespoon Lea & Perrins' Lemon and Herbs Sauce *or*
1 tablespoon Lea & Perrins' Chilli & Garlic Sauce *or*
1 tablespoon Lea & Perrins' Spiced Peppercorn Sauce
chopped parsley, chives or herbs of your choice.

1 Beat all the ingredients together in a bowl until thoroughly mixed.
2 Using cool, wet hands, shape the butter into a roll about 3 cm (1½ inches) in diameter.
3 Wrap in foil and refrigerate for immediate use or freeze.

✳ Suitable for freezing. To cut slices while frozen, use a knife dipped into hot water.

# FISH

## COD PROVENÇALE

*Serves 4*

---

4 frozen cod portions, thawed
juice of ½ lemon
2 tablespoons oil
1 small onion, peeled and finely chopped
1 clove of garlic, crushed
1 tablespoon plain flour
397 g (14 oz) can of tomatoes
2 tablespoons Worcestershire Sauce
1 tablespoon tomato purée
seasoning, to taste

1 Sprinkle the cod steaks with the lemon juice, season to taste, and leave for approximately half an hour.
2 Heat the oil in a large frying pan or shallow saucepan, and fry the onion and garlic gently, until transparent.
3 Stir in the flour and, when well mixed, add the tomatoes, Worcestershire Sauce and tomato purée. Bring to the boil, stirring all the time, and reduce the heat to simmering point.
4 Add the cod steaks to the pan, coat the fish with the sauce and gently simmer for approximately 20 minutes, stirring occasionally.
5 Taste and adjust seasoning.
6 Serve with mashed potatoes or rice.

**Variation:** replace the Worcestershire Sauce with Lea & Perrins' Chilli and Garlic Sauce.

❄ Suitable for freezing.

📖 Reheat from frozen.

# FISH MEUNIÈRE

*Serves 4*

---

4 medium-size plaice fillets
seasoned flour, for dusting
125 g (4 oz) butter
1 tablespoon Lea & Perrins' Lemon and Herbs Sauce

1  Rinse and dry the fillets and dust with a little seasoned flour.
2  Heat half of the butter and fry the fillets until golden (fleshy side first).
3  Transfer to a warmed serving dish and keep hot.
4  Heat the remaining butter in a clean pan until it just starts to turn pale brown, add the Lemon and Herbs Sauce and pour the foaming butter over the fish. Serve immediately.

*Fish Meunière*

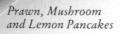

*Prawn, Mushroom and Lemon Pancakes*

*Cod Provençale*

# PRAWN, MUSHROOM AND LEMON PANCAKES

8–12 pancakes – made with your own favourite batter recipe, using 275 ml (½ pint) of milk
*For the filling:*
275 ml (½ pint) Basic White Sauce (page 6)
50 g (2 oz) mushrooms, washed, sliced, sautéd in butter and drained
175 g (6 oz) prawns
1 tablespoon Lea & Perrins' Lemon and Herbs Sauce
1 tablespoon chives, chopped
seasoning, to taste

1 Make the white sauce, remove from the heat and stir in the sautéd mushrooms, prawns, Lemon and Herbs Sauce, chopped chives and seasoning to taste.
2 Spread the pancakes with the filling and fold or roll up.
3 Place in a buttered ovenproof dish, cover and reheat in a fairly hot oven 200°C/400°F/Gas Mark 6 for 10–15 minutes.
4 Serve one per person as a starter or two as a main course.

❋ Suitable for freezing.

▤ Reheat from frozen.

# COD IN CAPER SAUCE

*Serves 4*

4 frozen cod steaks or portions
257 ml (½ pint) milk
25 g (1 oz) butter or margarine
25 g (1 oz) flour
2 tablespoons Lea & Perrins' Lemon and Herbs Sauce
70 g (2.5 oz) jar of capers, drained

1  Place the cod steaks in a pan with a little of the measured milk, and season with approximately 1 tablespoon of Lemon and Herbs Sauce.
2  Simmer gently, turning once, until the steaks are tender.
3  Drain the fish and keep warm, reserving the stock for the sauce.
4  To make the sauce, melt the butter in a saucepan, add the flour and stir for one minute.
5  Remove from the heat, add a little milk and blend well. Continue adding the milk and fish stock gradually and when smooth, return to the heat, and bring to the boil stirring constantly.
6  When the sauce has thickened, add the remaining tablespoon of Lemon and Herbs Sauce, and the capers.
7  Pour over the fish and serve immediately, accompanied by creamy mashed potatoes and fresh vegetables.

❄  Suitable for freezing.

▤  Reheat from frozen.

# FLAKY FISH PLAIT

225 g (8 oz) packet of frozen smoked haddock
198 g (7 oz) can of sweetcorn
1 teaspoon curry powder
1 tablespoon Worcestershire Sauce
1 tablespoon chopped parsley
seasoning, to taste
1 tablespoon soured cream
225 g (8 oz) packet of puff pastry, defrosted
2 tomatoes, skinned and sliced
beaten egg or milk, for glazing

1 Cook the smoked haddock according to instructions and flake with a fork, removing all skin and any bones.
2 In a bowl, combine the smoked haddock, sweetcorn, curry powder, Worcestershire Sauce and chopped parsley.
3 Season to taste and stir in the soured cream.
4 Roll out the pastry to a 25 cm (10 inch) square.
5 Arrange the mixture in a line down the centre and top with sliced tomatoes.
6 Cut the sides of the pastry into slanting strips about 2.5 cm (1 inch) wide, leaving 1.5 cm (½ inch) of pastry uncut on either side of the mixture.
7 Fold strips over the centre alternately from each side. Pinch the ends together and glaze the plait with beaten egg or milk.
8 Bake in an oven at 220°C/425°F/Gas Mark 7 for 25–30 minutes, or until the pastry is risen and golden brown.
9 Serve with a green salad or fresh vegetables.

**Variation:** replace the Worcestershire Sauce with Lea & Perrins' Lemon and Herbs Sauce.

❋ Suitable for freezing. Follow instructions as far as 7 but do not glaze. Freeze and then defrost at room temperature before glazing and cooking.

# LEMON AND HERB FISH CAKES

*Makes 8 fish cakes*

---

350 g (12 oz) cooked white fish, flaked
225 g (8 oz) mashed potatoes
25 g (1 oz) butter or margarine, melted
2 teaspoons parsley, finely chopped
1 egg, beaten
1 tablespoon Lea & Perrins' Lemon and Herbs Sauce
seasoning, to taste
*For the coating:*
1 egg, beaten
75 g (3 oz) breadcrumbs

1  Place the fish, potatoes, butter or margarine, parsley, egg and Lemon and Herbs Sauce in a bowl and gently mix together.
2  Taste, and adjust seasoning if necessary.
3  Chill the mixture in the refrigerator for 30 minutes.
4  Turn the mixture onto a floured surface and roll into a long cylinder shape.
5  Cut into 8 portions and shape each into a flat 'round'.
6  Dip the fish cakes into the beaten egg and then coat in the breadcrumbs.
7  Leave to chill in the refrigerator.
8  Fry in hot, shallow fat for 5 minutes on each side, or until golden brown and heated through.

❄ Suitable for freezing. Follow instructions to 6, freeze and fry the frozen fish cakes as above.

# PRAWN AND EGG FLAN

150 ml (¼ pint) Basic White Sauce (page 6)
125 g (4 oz) cottage cheese, sieved
125 g (4 oz) prawns
1 tablespoon Lea and Perrins' Spiced Peppercorn Sauce
1 hard boiled egg, chopped
seasoning, to taste
20 cm (8 inch) flan ring, lined with shortcrust pastry,
ready baked
50 g (2 oz) cheese, grated

1 To the Basic White Sauce add the sieved cottage cheese, prawns, Spiced Peppercorn Sauce, chopped egg and seasoning to taste.
2 Pour the mixture into the cooked flan case.
3 Sprinkle with the grated cheese and bake in a hot oven at 200°C/400°F/Gas Mark 6, until golden brown.
4 Remove the flan from the oven and allow to stand before serving. It is best served cold as a light lunch or supper snack.

**Variation:** replace the Spiced Peppercorn Sauce with Lea and Perrins' Chilli and Garlic or Worcestershire Sauce.

❄ Suitable for freezing.

▤ Reheat from frozen.

# SMOKED HADDOCK AND TOMATO FLAN

*For the pastry:*
50 g (2 oz) plain white flour
50 g (2 oz) wholemeal flour
50 g (2 oz) butter or margarine, cut into small pieces
approximately 1 tablespoon cold water
*For the filling:*
1 tablespoon oil
1 onion, peeled and chopped
225 g (8 oz) packet of smoked haddock, cooked, skinned and
flaked, removing all bones
2 tomatoes, skinned and chopped
2 eggs
150 ml (¼ pint) milk
1 tablespoon Worcestershire Sauce
seasoning, to taste
50 g (2 oz) cheese, grated

1  Sift the flours into a bowl and rub in the butter or margarine, using the fingertips, until it resembles fine crumbs.
2  Stir in sufficient water to mix to a stiff dough.
3  Wrap the pastry in foil and chill in the refrigerator for 30 minutes.
4  Roll out the pastry onto a floured working surface and use to line an 18 cm (7 inch) flan dish or flan ring.
5  Heat the oil, add the onion and fry until transparent.
6  Drain the onions and spoon into the pastry case, together with the haddock and tomatoes.
7  Place the eggs, milk and seasoning in a bowl, together with the Worcestershire Sauce, and beat together.
8  Pour into the flan and sprinkle with the grated cheese.
9  Bake the flan in a moderate oven, 180°C/350°F/Gas Mark 4, for 35 minutes or until the filling is set. Serve hot or cold.

**Variation:** Worcestershire Pastry – substitute one tablespoon of Worcestershire Sauce for the one tablespoon of added water.

❄ Suitable for freezing.

▤ Reheat from frozen.

# SARDINE AND LEMON PÂTÉ

*Serves 4–6*

---

50 g (2 oz) butter or margarine
75g (3 oz) fresh white or brown breadcrumbs
1 tablespoon Lea & Perrins' Lemon and Herbs Sauce
2 teaspoons finely chopped parsley
124 g (4.37 oz) can of sardines, boned and mashed with oil
seasoning, to taste

1 Melt the butter or margarine in a saucepan.
2 Remove from the heat and stir in the breadcrumbs, Lemon and Herbs Sauce, parsley and sardines.
3 Beat together until smooth, taste and adjust seasoning.
4 Spoon the mixture into a serving dish and chill before serving.
5 Serve with hot toast or crusty bread, either as a starter or a snack.

❄ Suitable for freezing.

*Sardine and Lemon Pâté*
*Smoked Haddock and Tomato Flan*

# SALMON AND SWEETCORN SALAD

*Serves 4*

1 green pepper, de-seeded
198 g (7 oz) can of salmon, drained and flaked
198 g (7 oz) can of sweetcorn kernels, drained
3 large carrots, grated
1 cucumber, sliced
8 tablespoons mayonnaise
2 tablespoons Worcestershire Sauce

1 Take several thin slices from the green pepper for garnish and chop the remainder.
2 Mix the salmon, sweetcorn, grated carrot and green pepper lightly together.
3 Line a shallow dish with overlapping cucumber slices and pile the salmon mixture in the centre.
4 Thin the mayonnaise with Worcestershire Sauce and pour over the salmon mixture.
5 Garnish with cucumber slices and pepper rings. Serve as a lunch or supper dish, with crusty bread or baked potatoes.

**Variations:** tuna fish can be used in place of the salmon. For an alternative flavour replace the Worcestershire Sauce with one of the three Lea & Perrins' Culinary Sauces – Chilli and Garlic, Lemon and Herbs or Spiced Peppercorn.

# TUNA SALAD

*Serves 4*

---

4 tablespoons mayonnaise
1 tablespoon Worcestershire Sauce
198 g (7 oz) can of tuna, drained and flaked
shredded lettuce
*To garnish:*
finely sliced cucumber
1 hard boiled egg, sliced

1 Mix the mayonnaise and Worcestershire Sauce to a smooth consistency; add the tuna and mix lightly together.
2 Arrange a bed of shredded lettuce on a serving dish.
3 Pour the tuna mixture onto the lettuce.
4 Garnish with slices of egg and cucumber.
5 Chill before serving as a first course or as a dressed salad for a light lunch or supper.

# SALAD NIÇOISE

*Serves 4*

4 tomatoes, quartered
½ spanish onion, sliced
1 green pepper, de-seeded and sliced
8 radishes, sliced
1 lettuce, washed and prepared
4 stalks of celery, sliced
198 g (7 oz) can of tuna, drained
2 hard boiled eggs, quartered
a few black olives (optional)
oil and vinegar dressing (page 12)

1 Combine all the prepared salad ingredients in a serving bowl.
2 Place chunks of tuna, the quartered eggs and the olives (if used) neatly on top of the salad ingredients.
3 Combine all the dressing ingredients, mix well and just before serving, sprinkle over the salad. Serve immediately, with crusty bread or rolls.

*Salad Niçoise*

# MEAT AND POULTRY

## BEEF CARBONADE

*Serves 4*                                    *180°C/350°F/Gas Mark 4*

---

700 g (1½ lb) lean braising steak, cut into 5 cm (2 inch) cubes
1 tablespoon flour
seasoning, to taste
25 g (1 oz) butter or margarine
1 tablespoon oil
3 large onions, peeled and thinly sliced
275 ml (½ pint) brown ale
275 ml (½ pint) beef stock
3 tablespoons Lea & Perrins' Spiced Peppercorn Sauce
french bread, sliced
french mustard

1 Coat the steak in the flour, with seasoning added, and reserve any remaining flour.
2 Heat the butter and oil in a pan, add the steak and fry briskly for 5 minutes; remove with a draining spoon and place in a casserole dish.
3 Add the onions to the pan and fry until transparent.
4 Sprinkle in the remaining flour and cook, stirring constantly.
5 Gradually stir in the brown ale, stock and Spiced Peppercorn Sauce and bring to the boil, stirring constantly.
6 Pour the sauce over the meat, cover the casserole and cook in a moderate oven at 180°C/350°F/Gas Mark 4 for 1½–2 hours or until the meat is tender.
7 Taste, and adjust seasoning if necessary.
8 Spread the slices of french bread with french mustard and place on top of the casserole.
9 Return the casserole, uncovered, to the oven for approximately 20–30 minutes until the bread is moist underneath and crisp on top. Serve immediately.

※ Ideal to freeze, following instructions to 7.

▤ Defrost before reheating and finishing with the french bread.

# MOUSSAKA

*Serves 6*          *190°C/375°F/Gas Mark 5*

700 g (1½ lb) aubergines, washed and cut into ½ cm (¼ inch) thick slices
75 ml (3 fl oz) oil
25 g (1 oz) butter
2 onions, peeled and sliced
1 clove of garlic, crushed
450 g (1 lb) lean minced beef
seasoning, to taste
1 tablespoon tomato purée
397 g (14 oz) can of tomatoes
1 tablespoon Worcestershire Sauce
275 ml (½ pint) Basic White Sauce (page 6)
1 egg yolk
125 g (4 oz) cottage cheese, sieved
25 g (1 oz) cheese, grated

1 Place the aubergine slices on a tray, sprinkle with salt and leave for 30 minutes. Drain off any liquid and dry on absorbent kitchen paper.
2 Heat the oil in a large frying pan and fry the aubergines until soft, adding more oil if necessary; remove from the pan and keep to one side.
3 Add the butter to the pan and fry the onion and garlic until soft and transparent; stir in the meat and seasoning and fry briskly.
4 When the meat is well browned (approximately 8 minutes), stir in the tomato purée, canned tomatoes and Worcestershire Sauce, bring to the boil and then remove from the heat.
5 Butter a deep casserole dish and fill with alternate layers of the aubergines and minced meat mixture, starting and ending with a layer of aubergines.
6 Make the Basic White Sauce, remove from the heat and add the egg yolk and sieved cottage cheese. Season to taste.
7 Pour the sauce over the casserole and sprinkle with the cheese.
8 Cook in a fairly hot oven at 190°C/375°F/Gas Mark 5 for 45–50 minutes.
9 Serve with crusty bread or pitta bread and a green salad.

❋ Suitable for freezing.

▤ Reheat from frozen.

Moussaka

*Meatballs with Peppers and Tomatoes*

*Beef Carbonade*

# MEATBALLS WITH PEPPERS AND TOMATOES

*For the meatballs:*
1 medium-size onion, finely chopped
½ green pepper, de-seeded and finely chopped
1 clove of garlic, crushed
1 tablespoon parsley, finely chopped
2 slices of bread, crust removed and crumbed
1 teaspoon dried, mixed herbs
2 teaspoons tomato purée
450 g (1 lb) lean minced beef
225 g (8 oz) pork sausage meat
1 egg
flour, to coat
oil, to shallow fry
*For the tomato sauce:*
1 small onion, finely chopped
½ green pepper, de-seeded and finely chopped
1 clove of garlic, crushed
397 g (14 oz) can of chopped tomatoes
1 tablespoon Worcestershire Sauce

1  In a large mixing bowl combine all the ingredients for the meatballs (except the flour and oil) and mix *very* thoroughly.
2  Take about a tablespoon at a time, form into a 'ball' and coat lightly with flour.
3  Heat the oil in a large pan and quickly brown the meatballs.
4  Drain, and transfer them to a casserole.
5  In the juices remaining in the pan, make the tomato sauce by frying the onion, pepper and garlic, adding the tomatoes and Worcestershire Sauce and simmering for approximately 5 minutes.
6  Pour the sauce over the meatballs, cover the casserole and cook in a fairly hot oven at 190°C/375°F/Gas Mark 5 for approximately 45 minutes.
7  Remove the lid and continue cooking for a further 20 minutes.
8  Serve with hot, buttered noodles or mashed or baked potatoes.

**Variation:** replace the Worcestershire Sauce with Lea & Perrins' Chilli and Garlic Sauce or Spiced Peppercorn Sauce.

❄ Suitable for freezing.

▤ Reheat from frozen.

# BEEF PROVENÇALE

2 tablespoons oil
450 g (1 lb) lean braising steak, trimmed and cut into 2.5 cm
(1 inch) cubes
2 medium-size onions, peeled and sliced
2 carrots, peeled and sliced
2 sticks of celery, cut into small pieces
½ green pepper, de-seeded and sliced
½ red pepper, de-seeded and sliced
397 g (14 oz) can of chopped tomatoes
1 tablespoon tomato purée
3 tablespoons Lea & Perrins' Spiced Peppercorn Sauce
125 g (4 oz) mushrooms, trimmed and sliced

1 Heat the oil in a pan and fry the steak until browned and sealed.
Drain and transfer to a casserole dish.
2 Fry in turn the onions, carrots, celery and green and red peppers.
3 Add the vegetables to the casserole and mix well with the meat.
4 Add the can of chopped tomatoes, the tomato purée and the Spiced
Peppercorn Sauce.
5 Mix well, cover the casserole and cook at 180°C/350°F/Gas Mark 4
for approximately 1¼ hours.
6 After this time, stir in the prepared mushrooms and continue to
cook for a further ½ hour.
7 Serve accompanied by jacket potatoes or crusty bread.

**Variation:** replace the Spiced Peppercorn Sauce with Worcestershire Sauce.

✳ Suitable for freezing.

▤ Reheat from frozen.

# CHILLI CON CARNE

*Serves 8*

---

225 g (8 oz) dried red kidney beans*, soaked overnight
4 tablespoons oil
2 onions, peeled and chopped
2 cloves of garlic, crushed
900 g (2 lb) lean minced beef
1 green pepper, de-seeded and chopped
3 tablespoons Lea & Perrins' Chilli and Garlic Sauce
1 teaspoon paprika pepper
1 teaspoon ground cumin
1 tablespoon tomato purée
1 tablespoon flour
seasoning, to taste
2 × 397 g (14 oz) can of tomatoes

1 Drain the kidney beans and cook gently in boiling salted water for 45 minutes or until tender. Drain and reserve about 150 ml (¼ pint) of the water.
2 Heat the oil in a saucepan, add the onion and garlic and fry until golden.
3 Add the beef and green pepper and fry for 5–6 minutes, stirring constantly to break up the meat.
4 Stir in the Chilli and Garlic Sauce, paprika, cumin, tomato purée, flour and seasoning to taste and cook for 2 minutes.
5 Add the tomatoes and the beans, mix thoroughly and bring to the boil, then lower the heat, cover and simmer on top of the stove for 1½ hours, stirring occasionally, to prevent the meat sticking. If it gets rather dry, add some of the reserved bean water.
6 Serve accompanied by brown rice or crusty bread.

*To save time, canned kidney beans can be used instead of dried. Just add 397 g (14 oz) can about 15 minutes before the end of the cooking time. When using dried beans, *always* follow the instructions on the packet *very* carefully.

❄ Suitable for freezing.
▤ Reheat from frozen.

# DUTCH BEEF STEW

*Serves 6*

---

900 g (2 lb) lean braising steak, cut into 5 cm (2 inch) cubes
*For the marinade:*
2 tablespoons malt vinegar
125 ml (4 fl oz) oil
1 tablespoon Worcestershire Sauce
seasoning, to taste
*For the stew:*
2 tablespoons oil
3 large onions, peeled and sliced
25 g (1 oz) flour
275 ml (½ pint) brown ale
150 ml (¼ pint) beef stock
1 tablespoon Worcestershire Sauce
pinch of sugar

1 Place the meat in a bowl and pour over the vinegar, oil, Worcestershire Sauce and seasoning. Allow the meat to marinate in the liquid for at least 2 hours.
2 Heat the oil in a heavy pan and fry the onions until lightly browned. Remove from the pan.
3 Add the meat to the pan, drained of the marinade, and fry briskly until brown and sealed.
4 Sprinkle in the flour and cook for 1 minute, stirring constantly.
5 Gradually stir in the ale, stock and Worcestershire Sauce and bring to the boil, stirring constantly.
6 Stir in the sugar, return the onions to the pan and season to taste.
7 Cover the pan, reduce the heat and simmer, stirring occasionally, for 1½–2 hours or until the meat is tender.
8 Serve with baked potatoes or crusty bread.

**Variation:** replace the Worcestershire Sauce with Lea & Perrins' Spiced Peppercorn Sauce.

❄ Suitable for freezing.

▤ Reheat from frozen.

# SPICY LAYER COTTAGE PIE

2 tablespoons oil
1 medium-size onion, peeled and finely chopped
2 cloves of garlic
450 g (1 lb) lean minced beef
2 tablespoons Worcestershire Sauce
397 g (14 oz) can of tomatoes
175 g (6 oz) leeks, finely sliced
175 g (6 oz) carrots, diced
4 sticks celery, thinly sliced
450 g (1 lb) potatoes
1 tablespoon finely chopped parsley
seasoning, to taste

1  Heat the oil and fry the onion, garlic and minced beef.
2  When the meat is well browned, add the Worcestershire Sauce and the can of tomatoes.
3  Simmer rapidly until the liquid is absorbed.
4  Meanwhile, parboil the leeks, carrots and celery for approximately 5 minutes and boil the potatoes for the topping.
5  Put a layer of the mixed vegetables on the base of a casserole dish, cover with half the meat mixture and another layer of vegetables.
6  Repeat the layers finishing with a layer of vegetables.
7  Mash and season the potatoes, add the chopped parsley and spoon or pipe onto the top of the pie.
8  Cook in a moderate oven at 180°C/350°F/Gas Mark 4 for approximately 45 minutes.

**Variations:** replace the Worcestershire Sauce with Lea & Perrins' Chilli and Garlic Sauce. Other cooked, leftover vegetables may be substituted for the leeks, carrots and celery.

✳  Suitable for freezing.

▤  Reheat from frozen.

# BEEFBURGERS WITH ORANGE BARBECUED SAUCE

*Serves 4*                                          *170°C/325°F/Gas Mark 3*

4 beefburgers
2 medium-size onions, peeled and sliced
*For the sauce:*
1 tablespoon oil
15 g (½ oz) butter
1 teaspoon flour
150 ml (¼ pint) orange juice (fresh or canned)
1 teaspoon finely grated orange rind (optional)
1 tablespoon Worcestershire Sauce
1 tablespoon tomato purée
4 canned tomatoes, drained
seasoning, to taste

1  Brown the beefburgers and sauté the onions gently in the oil.
2  Place in a casserole.
3  Make a roux with the butter and flour by melting the butter
and stirring in the flour; gradually stir in the orange juice,
Worcestershire Sauce and tomato purée, and bring the sauce to
the boil, stirring all the time.
4  Cook well, stir in the tomatoes and season to taste.
5  Pour the sauce into the casserole and cook for 30 minutes at
170°C/325°F/Gas Mark 3.
6  Taste, adjust seasoning, and garnish with strips of orange rind.
7  Serve, garnished with segments of fresh orange, with baked
potatoes and a crisp, green salad.

**Variation:** try using pork chops instead of beefburgers.

❋  Suitable for freezing.

▤  Reheat from frozen.

# SWEET AND SOUR PORK SPARE RIBS

*Serves 4*                    *220°C/425°F/Gas Mark 7*
                              *180°C/350°F/Gas Mark 4*

---

1 kg (2 lb) pork spare ribs
1 tablespoon oil
1 onion, peeled and chopped
1 small carrot, peeled and cut into thin strips
150 ml (¼ pint) pineapple juice
75 ml (3 fl oz) white wine vinegar
2 tablespoons Worcestershire Sauce
50 g (2 oz) soft brown sugar
1 tablespoon cornflour
4 tablespoons water
juice and grated rind of ½ lemon
seasoning, to taste

1 Place the spare ribs in a baking tin and cook uncovered in a hot oven at 220°C/425°F/Gas Mark 7 for 20 minutes.
2 Remove the ribs, drain off any fat, wipe the tin and replace the ribs in it.
3 Heat the oil in a pan, add the onions and carrot and fry for 5 minutes.
4 Pour in the pineapple juice, vinegar, Worcestershire Sauce and brown sugar and stir until the sugar has dissolved.
5 Lower the heat and simmer for 20 minutes, stirring occasionally. Remove from the heat.
6 Blend the cornflour and water together in a jug until smooth, and add to the sauce, together with the lemon juice, rind and seasoning to taste.
7 Return to the heat, bring to the boil, stirring constantly, then simmer until thick.
8 Pour the sauce over the spare ribs, cover and cook in a moderate oven at 180°C/350°F/Gas Mark 4 for 40 minutes.
9 Baste the ribs with the sauce two to three times during the cooking time.
10 Serve immediately, with brown rice and a salad.

❄ Suitable for freezing.

▤ Reheat from frozen.

*Sweet and Sour Pork Spare Ribs*
*Pork Chops in Orange Sauce*

# PORK CHOPS IN ORANGE SAUCE

*Serves 4*

---

4 boneless pork chops
25 g (1 oz) butter or margarine
*For the sauce:*
2 teaspoons cornflour
juice from 1 large orange (approximately 8 tablespoons)
150 ml (¼ pint) chicken stock
2 tablespoons Lea & Perrins' Lemon and Herbs Sauce
seasoning, to taste
*To garnish:*
1 orange, peeled, pith removed and segmented

1 Heat the butter in a pan and brown the chops on both sides.
2 Remove the chops and drain on absorbent kitchen paper.
3 Mix the cornflour with a little orange juice, blend and add the remaining juice, stock, Lemon and Herbs Sauce and seasoning.
4 Transfer to the pan and bring to the boil stirring constantly.
5 Return the chops to the pan, reduce the heat, cover and simmer gently for approximately 30–40 minutes, or until tender.
6 Garnish with orange segments 5 minutes before serving.
7 Serve with mashed, new or baked potatoes and fresh vegetables.

**Variation:** replace the Lemon and Herbs Sauce with Worcestershire Sauce.

❄ Suitable for freezing.

▤ Reheat from frozen.

# PORK KEBABS

*Serves 4*

---

575 g (1¼ lb) pork fillet, trimmed and cut into about 20 cubes
275 ml (½ pint) Honey and Pineapple Marinade (page 11)
4 pineapple rings, cut into pieces
1 large green pepper, de-seeded and cut into pieces
1 teaspoon cornflour

1 Pour the marinade over the meat and leave for at least 2 hours.
2 Drain well, reserving the marinade, and using 4 large or 8 small skewers, thread alternate pieces of meat, pepper and pineapple onto each skewer.
3 Grill under a medium/high grill, turning regularly to ensure thorough cooking. Alternatively, cook on a barbecue.
4 Meanwhile, mix the cornflour with the marinade and bring to the boil. Either serve the sauce separately or poured over the kebabs on a bed of rice.

# FOIL WRAPPED LAMB

*Serves 4*                                    *190°C/375°F/Gas Mark 5*

4 lamb loin chops, trimmed of excess fat
2 tablespoons flour, seasoned
50 g (2 oz) butter or margarine
2 onions, peeled and cut into rings
1 clove of garlic, crushed
397 g (14 oz) can of chopped tomatoes
1½ tablespoons Worcestershire Sauce
2 teaspoons chopped parsley
seasoning, to taste

1 Toss the chops in seasoned flour. Melt the butter or margarine in a frying pan and briskly fry the chops until golden brown on both sides.
2 Remove, drain and place each chop on a large square of heavy duty or double layered foil.
3 Add the onions and garlic to the pan and cook for about 2 minutes.
4 Stir in the chopped tomatoes and Worcestershire Sauce. Season, and simmer until the mixture reduces and is thick in consistency.
5 Remove from the heat and stir in the chopped parsley.
6 Divide the mixture equally between the 4 lamb chops, spreading it over the top of them.
7 Fold the foil loosely to make parcels and seal the edges securely.
8 Place the parcels on a baking sheet and put into a fairly hot oven (190°C/375°F/Gas mark 5) for 35–40 minutes, or until the chops are cooked and tender. Serve immediately in the foil.

**Variation:** replace the Worcestershire Sauce with Chilli & Garlic Sauce or Spiced Peppercorn Sauce.

❄ Suitable for freezing.

# LAMB IN COURGETTES AND TOMATOES

*Serves 4*

oil or butter, for frying
1 onion, peeled and finely chopped
4 loin lamb chops, trimmed of excess fat
flour, for coating
397 g (14 oz) can of chopped tomatoes
2 tablespoons tomato purée
3 tablespoons Lea & Perrins' Chilli and Garlic Sauce
225 g (½ lb) courgettes, sliced

1 Heat the oil or butter, add the onion and fry until golden.
2 Coat the lamb chops lightly in flour, add to the pan and brown quickly on both sides.
3 Stir in the canned tomatoes, tomato purée, Chilli and Garlic Sauce and courgettes.
4 Bring to the boil, cover and simmer for approximately 45 minutes, turning the chops once during cooking.
5 When the lamb chops are tender, serve immediately, with jacket potatoes or wholemeal pasta.

**Variation:** replace the Chilli and Garlic Sauce with Worcestershire Sauce.

❄ Suitable for freezing.

▤ Reheat from frozen.

*Lamb in Courgettes and Tomatoes*

# SPICY BRAISED KIDNEYS

*Serves 4–5*

---

75 g (3 oz) butter or margarine
10 lamb's kidneys, skinned, halved and cored
1 onion, peeled and finely chopped
125 g (4 oz) mushrooms, washed and thickly sliced
50 g (2 oz) flour
425 ml (¾ pint) beef stock
1 tablespoon Worcestershire Sauce
seasoning, to taste
parsley, to garnish

1 Melt the butter or margarine in a pan, add the kidneys and fry briskly for 5 minutes. Remove from the pan.
2 Add the onions to the pan and fry until transparent.
3 Add the mushrooms and cook for 2 minutes.
4 Sprinkle in the flour and cook, stirring constantly, for 1 minute.
5 Gradually stir in the stock and Worcestershire Sauce and bring to the boil, stirring constantly.
6 Add the kidneys, season to taste, reduce the heat and simmer for 10 minutes.
7 Garnish with a little chopped parsley and serve accompanied by brown rice or mashed potatoes.

**Variation:** replace the Worcestershire Sauce with Lea & Perrins' Spiced Peppercorn Sauce.

❄ Suitable for freezing.

▤ Reheat from frozen.

# LIVER HOT POT

450 g (1 lb) calves' or lamb's liver, well trimmed and thinly sliced
25 g (1 oz) flour
seasoning, to taste
25 g (1 oz) butter or margarine
4 rashers lean bacon, de-rinded and chopped
2 large onions, peeled and sliced
275 ml (½ pint) beef stock
2 teaspoons tomato ketchup
1 tablespoon Worcestershire Sauce
1 tablespoon finely chopped parsley

1 Toss the liver in the seasoned flour, reserving any leftover flour.
2 Heat the butter or margarine in a pan, add the liver and fry briskly for 2 minutes, then transfer to an ovenproof dish.
3 Add the bacon and onion to the pan and fry until golden brown.
4 Sprinkle in any leftover flour and cook for 1 minute, stirring constantly.
5 Gradually stir in the stock, ketchup, and Worcestershire Sauce and bring to the boil, stirring constantly.
6 Remove from the heat, stir in the parsley, taste and adjust seasoning if necessary.
7 Pour the sauce over the liver, cover the casserole and bake in a moderate oven at 180°C/350°F/Gas Mark 4 for 20–30 minutes.
8 Serve with baked or mashed potatoes and fresh vegetables.

**Variation:** replace the Worcestershire Sauce with Spiced Peppercorn Sauce.

❄ Suitable for freezing.

▤ Reheat from frozen.

# CHICKEN MORNAY

*Serves 4*                                        *200°C/400°F/Gas Mark 6*

450 g (1 lb) cooked chicken, cut into bite-size pieces
275 ml (½ pint) Basic White Sauce (page 6)
50 g (2 oz) cheese, grated
2 tablespoons Lea & Perrins' Spiced Peppercorn Sauce
*For the topping:*
ready salted crisps, crushed
25 g (1 oz) cheese, grated

1 Put the prepared chicken into an ovenproof dish.
2 Make the white sauce, and add the grated cheese and Spiced Pepper-corn Sauce.
3 Pour the sauce over the chicken, sprinkle the crushed crisps and grated cheese evenly over the top and put into a fairly hot oven (200°C/400°F/Gas Mark 6).
4 Serve when heated through and golden brown on top (approximately 20 minutes).

**Variation:** replace the Spiced Peppercorn Sauce with Worcestershire Sauce.

*Chicken and Mushroom Vol-au-Vents*

*Chicken with Peaches*

*Chicken Mornay*

49

# CHICKEN WITH PEACHES

*Serves 4*

---

50 g (2 oz) butter or margarine
1 tablespoon oil
4 chicken portions
2 onions, peeled and sliced
25 g (1 oz) flour
1 tablespoon curry powder
½ teaspoon ground ginger
½ teaspoon ground cinnamon
275 ml (½ pint) chicken stock
1 tablespoon mango chutney
2 fresh peaches, skinned and stoned *or* 4 canned peach halves, drained
2 tablespoons Lea & Perrins' Lemon and Herbs Sauce

1 Heat the butter and oil in a large pan, add the chicken joints and fry until crisp and golden on both sides. Remove from the pan and keep to one side.
2 Add the onions to the pan and fry until soft.
3 Sprinkle in the flour, curry powder, ginger and cinnamon and cook for 1 minute, stirring constantly.
4 Gradually stir in the chicken stock and bring to the boil, stirring constantly.
5 When the sauce has thickened, add the mango chutney.
6 Return the chicken portions to the curry sauce, cover the pan, reduce the heat and simmer for approximately one hour.
7 Add the peaches and Lemon and Herbs Sauce.
8 Simmer for a further 5 minutes and serve with brown rice and a side dish of sliced cucumber in plain yogurt.

❄ Suitable for freezing.

▤ Reheat from frozen.

# CHICKEN AND MUSHROOM VOL-AU-VENTS

225 g (8 oz) frozen puff pastry, thawed
beaten egg, to glaze
*For the filling:*
275 ml (½ pint) Basic White Sauce (page 6)
1 tablespoon Lea & Perrins' Chilli and Garlic Sauce
25 g (1 oz) butter or margarine
125 g (4 oz) mushrooms, washed and sliced
175 g (6 oz) chicken, cut into small pieces
seasoning, to taste

1 Roll the pastry out to ½ cm (¼ inch) thickness on a floured board.
2 Cut the pastry into four circles using a 9 cm (3½ inch) pastry cutter
and place on a damp baking tray.
3 Cut halfway through the centre of each circle with a 5 cm (2 inch)
pastry cutter.
4 Brush with beaten egg and bake in the centre of a hot oven at
220°C/425°F/Gas Mark 7 for 20 minutes, or until well risen and crisp.
Allow to cool, and with a sharp knife, carefully remove the pastry lids,
keeping them to one side.
5 Make the white sauce, remove from the heat, season and add the
Chilli and Garlic Sauce.
6 Sauté the mushrooms in the butter or margarine, drain and add to
the sauce with the chicken. Stir well.
7 Divide the mixture between the pastry cases, replace the lids and
serve, garnished with a little parsley or watercress.

**Variations:** replace the Chilli and Garlic Sauce with Lemon and
Herbs Sauce. For a party, make small, individual vol-au-vent cases
instead of the larger ones.

# STIR-FRIED HOT SPICED CHICKEN WITH PEPPERS

*Serves 4*

2 tablespoons oil
275 g (10 oz) chicken breasts, cut into thin strips
½ green pepper, de-seeded and cut into very fine strips
½ red pepper, de-seeded and cut into very fine strips
*For the sauce:*
2 teaspoons cornflour
3 tablespoons stock
1 tablespoon vinegar
1 tablespoon tomato purée
1 tablespoon sherry
2 tablespoons Lea & Perrins' Chilli and Garlic Sauce

1 Heat the oil in a wok or frying pan, add the chicken strips and stir-fry briskly for 2 minutes.
2 Remove the chicken and drain. Add the peppers to the oil and stir-fry briskly for 2 minutes.
4 Combine all the sauce ingredients, pour into the pan, and bring to the boil, stirring constantly.
5 Add the chicken pieces, continue to cook the mixture for about 1 minute and serve, accompanied by stir-fried vegetables and rice or noodles.

**Variations:** pork fillet cut into thin strips may be used as an alternative to chicken. Try replacing the Chilli and Garlic Sauce with Worcestershire Sauce for a different flavour.

*Stir-fried Hot Spiced Chicken with Peppers*

# CHICKEN PROVENÇALE

*Serves 4*

2 tablespoons oil
4 chicken portions
2 onions, peeled and finely chopped
2 cloves of garlic, crushed
1 green pepper, de-seeded and sliced
1 red pepper, de-seeded and sliced
397 g (14 oz) can of chopped tomatoes
1 tablespoon tomato purée
3 tablespoons Lea & Perrins' Spiced Peppercorn Sauce
seasoning, to taste

1 Heat the oil in a pan, add the chicken portions and fry them on both sides until golden brown.
2 Remove the chicken and drain on absorbent paper.
3 Add the onions, garlic and peppers to the pan and fry for approximately 3 minutes.
4 Add the tomatoes, tomato purée and Spiced Peppercorn Sauce, bring to the boil and reduce to a simmer.
5 Return the chicken joints to the pan, cover and cook for approximately 45 minutes or until the chicken is tender. Taste, and adjust seasoning if necessary.
6 Serve with rice, noodles or baked potatoes.

**Variation:** replace the Spiced Peppercorn Sauce with Worcestershire Sauce.

❄ Suitable for freezing.

☰ Reheat from frozen.

# CHICKEN, PINEAPPLE AND PASTA

*Serves 6*

450 g (1 lb) cooked chicken, cut into bite-size pieces
3 tablespoons oil
2 tablespoons Worcestershire Sauce
225 g (8 oz) wholemeal short cut macaroni
275 ml (½ pint) soured cream
2 tablespoons horseradish sauce
2 tablespoons tomato ketchup
1 tablespoon Worcestershire Sauce
225 g (8 oz) celery, sliced
350 g (12 oz) can of pineapple cubes, drained
25 g (1 oz) peanuts, to garnish

1 Marinate the chicken in the oil and two tablespoons of Worcestershire Sauce for approximately 1 hour.
2 Meanwhile, cook and drain the macaroni, according to packet instructions.
3 Mix the soured cream, horseradish sauce, tomato ketchup and one tablespoon of Worcestershire Sauce together.
4 Carefully fold in the cooled macaroni.
5 Add the celery and pineapple, mix carefully and combine with the marinated chicken.
6 Chill, and garnish with peanuts. Serve on a bed of lettuce with crusty bread, rolls or baked potatoes.

**Variations:** replace the Worcestershire Sauce with Lea & Perrins' Chilli and Garlic Sauce or Lea & Perrins' Spiced Peppercorn Sauce.

# BARBECUED CHICKEN WINGS

*Makes approximately 16 wings*

---

1.1 kg (2½ lb) chicken wings
*For the marinade:*
200 g (7 oz) bottle of tomato ketchup
2 tablespoons brown sugar
3 tablespoons Worcestershire Sauce
2 cloves of garlic, crushed

1 Wipe and trim the wings and remove wing tips.
2 Mix together the tomato ketchup, brown sugar, Worcestershire Sauce and crushed garlic, for the marinade.
3 Place the wings in a shallow container, pour the marinade over them and leave for at least 2 hours in a cool place.
4 Barbecue or grill the chicken wings, basting with the excess marinade and turning frequently, until crisp and well cooked. If barbecued, do ensure that they are *well* cooked all the way through.
5 Serve hot or cold, with salad and baked potatoes.

**Variation:** try this barbecue recipe using beefburgers, chops and other cuts of chicken.

*Barbecued Chicken Wings*
*Chicken, Pineapple and Pasta*

# Paprika Chicken

oil, for frying
2 large onions, peeled and finely chopped
2 cloves of garlic, crushed
4 chicken portions, skinned
1 tablespoon sweet mild paprika
seasoning, to taste
1 tablespoon Worcestershire Sauce, made up to 75 ml (3 fl oz)
with water
150 ml (5 fl oz) carton soured cream
chopped chives, to garnish

1 Heat the oil in a large frying pan, add the onions and garlic and gently cook on a low heat until golden in colour and soft in texture.
2 Increase the heat, add the chicken portions and brown on both sides.
3 Sprinkle in the paprika, seasoning and the Worcestershire stock.
4 Stir well and spoon the mixture over the chicken joints. Cover and cook gently for approximately 35–45 minutes (the onion purée should just 'coat' the chicken).
5 Spoon the soured cream and chives over the chicken.
6 Serve with brown rice or jacket potatoes.

**Variation:** replace the Worcestershire Sauce with Lea & Perrins' Chilli and Garlic Sauce.

❄ Suitable for freezing.

▤ Reheat from frozen.

# CHICKEN CROQUETTES

*Makes 8*

---

25 g (1 oz) flour
25 g (1 oz) butter or margarine
150 ml (¼ pint milk)
350 g (12 oz) cooked chicken, finely chopped
125 g (4 oz) mushrooms, washed and finely chopped
1 tablespoon freshly chopped parsley
1 tablespoon Worcestershire Sauce
flour, for coating
beaten egg, for coating
175 g (6 oz) breadcrumbs
oil, for deep fat frying

1  Make the white sauce using the flour, butter or margarine and milk, following the instructions for Basic White Sauce (page 6).
2  Mix together the chicken, mushrooms, white sauce, parsley and Worcestershire sauce.
3  Divide the mixture into eight, and with floured hands, shape into 'croquettes'.
4  Dip each croquette into beaten egg, coat in breadcrumbs and chill for one hour before frying.
5  Fry in deep fat for approximately 10 minutes, until crisp and golden. The fat should reach 190°C/375°F.
6  Drain, garnish with chopped parsley and lemon wedges and serve.

**Variation:** replace the Worcestershire Sauce with Lea & Perrins' Lemon and Herbs Sauce.

❄ Suitable for freezing, uncooked. Fry from frozen.

# VEGETABLE DISHES

## CABBAGE AU GRATIN

*Serves 4–6*                    *200°C/400°F/Gas Mark 6*

---

700 g (1½ lb) white cabbage, washed and trimmed
275 ml (½ pint) Basic White Sauce (page 6)
2 tablespoons Lea & Perrins' Spiced Peppercorn Sauce
2 tablespoons single cream
50 g (2 oz) cheese, grated
seasoning, to taste
25 g (1 oz) breadcrumbs
15 g (½ oz) margarine or butter

1 Shred the cabbage in ½ cm (¼ inch) slices and cook in boiling water for 5 minutes. Drain well.
2 Make the white sauce and flavour with the Lea & Perrins' Spiced Peppercorn Sauce. Remove from the heat and add the cream, grated cheese and seasoning, to taste.
3 Add the cabbage and stir well.
4 Turn into a buttered dish, sprinkle with the breadcrumbs and dot with the butter or margarine.
5 Put into a hot oven at 200°C/400°F/Gas Mark 6 for 30 minutes.

❄ Suitable for freezing.

▤ Reheat from frozen.

# BAKED POTATOES WITH CHEESE AND BACON

4 large old potatoes, scrubbed and wiped dry
1 tablespoon oil
50 g (2 oz) cheese, grated
75 g (3 oz) butter
seasoning, to taste
8 rashers of lean bacon
1 small onion, peeled and thinly sliced
2 large tomatoes, skinned and chopped
2 tablespoons Worcestershire Sauce
sprigs of parsley, to garnish

1 Place the potatoes on a baking tray, and prick with a fork. Rub the skins with a little oil and bake in a fairly hot oven at 200°C/400°F/Gas Mark 6 for 1½ hours or until cooked.
2 Halve the potatoes lengthways, scoop out the potato carefully, and mash in a bowl with the cheese, 75 g (2 oz) of the butter and seasoning.
3 Return the mixture to the potato cases, on the baking tray.
4 With four of the rashers of bacon, make eight bacon rolls and secure them with cocktail sticks. Place on the baking tray with the potatoes and return to the oven.
5 Chop the remaining bacon and fry it with the onion in 25 g (1 oz) of butter; stir in the tomatoes and Worcestershire Sauce.
6 Simmer for approximately 5 minutes and, when cooked, spoon onto the individual potatoes and garnish with a bacon roll and parsley.

▤ Cook the potatoes in your microwave and just top with the tomato and bacon mixture, which can be quickly stir-fried while the potatoes are cooking.

# CAULIFLOWER AND BACON SAVOURY

*Serves 4–6*

---

1 large cauliflower, washed, trimmed and broken into florets
25 g (1 oz) butter or margarine
1 onion, peeled and finely chopped
4 lean bacon rashers, chopped
50 g (2 oz) mushrooms, sliced
1 tablespoon Worcestershire Sauce
275 ml (½ pint) Basic White Sauce (page 6)
125 g (4 oz) cheese, grated
*To garnish:*
sprigs of parsley
tomato wedges

1 Cook the cauliflower florets in boiling water until tender.
2 Meanwhile, melt the butter or margarine and fry the onion in it until transparent.
3 Add the chopped bacon and fry for 1–2 minutes, then add the mushrooms and finally the Worcestershire Sauce. Simmer rapidly until all the liquid has been absorbed.
4 When the cauliflower is cooked, arrange the florets in a shallow dish, sprinkle the drained bacon mixture evenly over it and keep warm, while making the white sauce.
5 Remove the saucepan from the heat and stir in 50 g (2 oz) of the grated cheese.
6 Pour the sauce over the cauliflower, sprinkle with the remaining cheese and put under a very hot grill until the cheese bubbles and is golden brown.
7 Garnish with a little parsley and tomato and serve immediately.

❊ Suitable for freezing.

▤ Reheat from frozen.

# STUFFED GREEN PEPPERS

*Serves 4, or 8 as a first course*          *200°C/400°F/Gas Mark 6*

125 g (4 oz) long grain rice
1 tablespoon oil
125 g (4 oz) lean bacon, de-rinded and chopped
3 large tomatoes, skinned and chopped
1 clove of garlic, crushed
1 tablespoon Worcestershire Sauce
seasoning, to taste
4 medium-size green peppers
50g (2 oz) Cheddar cheese, grated

1  Cook the rice according to the instructions on the packet. Rinse and drain thoroughly.
2  Meanwhile, heat the oil in a pan, add the bacon and fry until crisp. Add the tomatoes, garlic, Worcestershire Sauce and rice.
3  Stir well and season to taste.
4  Cut the peppers in half lengthways, remove the seeds and membrane from the inside of the pepper, blanch in boiling water for 5 minutes and drain.
5  Place the peppers in a buttered dish and fill with the rice mixture.
6  Sprinkle with the cheese and cook at 200°C/400°F/Gas Mark 6 for approximately 25 minutes.

**Variation:** replace the Worcestershire Sauce with Lea & Perrins' Chilli and Garlic Sauce or Spiced Peppercorn Sauce.

❋  Suitable for freezing.

▤  Reheat from frozen.

# COURGETTES PROVENÇALE

*Serves 4*

2 tablespoons oil
450 g (1 lb) courgettes, washed, topped and tailed and cut into
1 cm (½ inch) slices
6 spring onions, washed, topped and tailed and roughly chopped
1 clove of garlic, crushed
4 tomatoes, skinned and chopped
1 tablespoon tomato purée
½ tablespoon Worcestershire Sauce
seasoning, to taste

1 Heat the oil in a pan, add the courgettes, spring onions and garlic
and cook for 3 minutes.
2 Stir in the remaining ingredients and season to taste.
3 Bring to the boil, cover and reduce the heat.
4 Simmer for approximately 15–20 minutes, stirring occasionally and
adding a little water if required.
5 When the courgettes are tender, serve immediately, either cold as a
starter or hot as a vegetable accompaniment to any roast or grilled
meat.

Suitable for freezing.

Reheat from frozen.

Cauliflower and
Bacon Savoury

# POTATO SALAD SPECIAL

*Serves 4*

---

575 g (1¼ lb) new potatoes, well cleaned but skins left on
125 ml (4 fl oz) mayonnaise
1 tablespoon Lea & Perrins' Spiced Peppercorn Sauce
198 g (7 oz) can of sweetcorn, drained
1 bunch of radishes, sliced (reserve two whole, for garnish)
1 bunch of spring onions, chopped

1  Cook the new potatoes until tender.
2  Drain and cool and cut into even-size pieces.
3  Mix the mayonnaise and Spiced Peppercorn Sauce until smooth.
4  Add the sweetcorn, sliced radishes and spring onions to the potatoes and gently coat with the Spiced Peppercorn dressing.
5  Refrigerate for at least one hour. Serve garnished with radish 'roses'.

# SWEETCORN AND HAM FLAN

*Serves 4–6*                                    *200°C/400°F/Gas Mark 6*

---

25 g (1 oz) butter or margarine
1 medium-size onion, peeled and chopped
275 ml (½ pint) Basic White Sauce (page 6)
75 g (3 oz) cheese, grated
175 g (6 oz) sweetcorn
125 g (4 oz) cooked ham, diced
1 tablespoon Worcestershire Sauce
20 cm (8 inch) flan ring, lined with shortcrust pastry, already baked

1  Melt the butter and fry the onion gently for a few minutes.
2  Add the drained onions to the white sauce, together with 50 g (2 oz) of the grated cheese, sweetcorn, ham and Worcestershire Sauce.
3  Pour the mixture into the flan case, sprinkle with the remaining grated cheese and bake in a hot oven at 200°C/400°F/Gas Mark 6 until golden brown.
4  Remove from the oven and allow to stand before serving.

▧ Suitable for freezing.
▤ Reheat from frozen.

# CRUNCHY SAVOURY PANCAKES

*Serves 4–6*

8–12 pancakes – made with your own favourite batter recipe,
using 275 ml (½ pint) milk
*For the filling:*
1 bunch of spring onions, chopped
3 tomatoes, skinned and chopped
2 sticks of celery, finely chopped
50 g (2 oz) mushrooms, sliced
½ green or red pepper, de-seeded and chopped
25 g (1 oz) butter or margarine
1 tablespoon Worcestershire Sauce
*For the sauce:*
275 ml (½ pint) Basic White Sauce (page 6)
125 g (4 oz) cheese, grated
seasoning, to taste
*To garnish:*
tomato wedges
a little chopped parsley

1 Make the pancakes and keep them warm.
2 To prepare the filling, melt the butter or margarine in a frying pan
and stir-fry all the vegetables.
3 Add the Worcestershire Sauce and simmer for 3 minutes.
4 Fill the prepared pancakes, roll them up and put in a oven proof
dish. Keep warm.
5 Make the white sauce.
6 Remove saucepan from the heat and stir in 50 g (2 oz) of the cheese.
7 Pour the sauce over the pancakes, sprinkle with the remaining cheese
and put under a very hot grill until the cheese bubbles and is golden
brown. Garnish with a little tomato and parsley and serve immediately.

Make a quantity of pancakes to freeze. Experiment with fillings such
as prawns, ham and cooked chicken.

❄ Suitable for freezing.
▤ Reheat from frozen.

# CHINESE BRAISED VEGETABLES

*Serves 4*

2 tablespoons oil
2 sticks of celery washed, trimmed and diced
2 carrots, peeled and cut into very fine strips
½ green pepper, de-seeded and cut into very fine strips
½ red pepper, de-seeded and cut into very fine strips
1 bunch of spring onions, trimmed and roughly chopped
½ cauliflower, washed and broken into very small florets
225 g (8 oz) beansprouts (optional)*
6 canned waterchestnuts, sliced (optional)*
125 g (4 oz) mushrooms, washed and sliced
75 ml (3 fl oz) water
1 teaspoon brown sugar
1 tablespoon Worcestershire Sauce
seasoning, to taste

1 Heat the oil in a wok or large saucepan or frying pan.
2 Add the celery and carrots, and stir-fry for 1–2 minutes.
3 Stir in the remaining vegetables a little at a time. Once all have been added, stir constantly for 2 minutes.
4 Add the water, brown sugar, Worcestershire Sauce and seasoning to taste, cook briskly, stirring occasionally, for approximately 5 minutes, or until the vegetables are cooked but still crisp.

**Variation:** replace the Worcestershire Sauce with Lea & Perrins' Chilli and Garlic Sauce.

* The more specialised foods such as beansprouts and waterchestnuts can be omitted if not available. All vegetables must be finely and evenly cut to ensure even cooking.

*Chinese Braised Vegetables*

# SPANISH RICE

*Serves 4*

175 g (6 oz) long grain rice
1 onion, peeled and finely sliced
1 green pepper, de-seeded and finely sliced
1 tablespoon oil
397 g (14 oz) can of tomatoes
1 tablespoon Worcestershire Sauce
seasoning, to taste
25–50 g (1–2 oz) grated parmesan cheese

1 Cook the rice according to the instructions on the packet. When cooked, rinse and drain thoroughly.
2 Meanwhile, heat the oil in a pan and sauté the onion and green pepper for about 5 minutes, or until soft.
3 Stir in the tomatoes with their juice, the Worcestershire Sauce and cooked rice.
4 Simmer, uncovered, for about 15 minutes, stirring occasionally to prevent burning.
5 Season to taste and sprinkle with the grated cheese.
6 Serve as an accompaniment to chops, steaks and beefburgers.

**Variation:** add some cooked meat or fish to the rice and serve it as a complete meal.

# WHOLEMEAL TOMATO QUICHE

*Serves 4–6*

*200°C/400°F/Gas Mark 6*
*180°C/350°F/Gas Mark 4*

*For the pastry:*
50 g (2 oz) plain white flour
50 g (2 oz) wholemeal flour
50 g (2 oz) butter or margarine, cut into small pieces
approximately 1 tablespoon cold water
*For the filling:*
125 g (4 oz) spring onions, trimmed and roughly chopped
1 tablespoon oil
4 firm tomatoes
1 egg
3 tablespoons natural yogurt
1 tablespoon Worcestershire Sauce
seasoning, to taste

1 Sift the flours into a bowl and rub in the butter or margarine, using the fingertips, until it resembles fine crumbs.
2 Stir in sufficient water to mix to a stiff dough.
3 Wrap in foil and chill in the refrigerator for 30 minutes.
4 Roll out the pastry onto a floured working surface and use to line an 18 cm (7 inch) flan ring or flan dish.
5 Bake blind in the oven at 200°C/400°F/Gas Mark 6 for about 15 minutes.
6 Fry the spring onions in the oil and drain.
7 Skin the tomatoes and cut into slices.
8 Arrange the tomatoes in overlapping circles in the base of the flan case and scatter the spring onions over the top.
9 Lightly whisk the egg, yogurt, seasoning and Worcestershire Sauce together and spoon carefully into the pastry case.
10 Bake at 180°C/350°F/Gas Mark 4 for 35–40 minutes, or until just set. Serve warm.

**Variations:** add a little chopped parsley or chives to the yogurt mixture, if available. For an alternative flavour replace the Worcestershire Sauce with Lea & Perrins' Chilli and Garlic Sauce or Spiced Peppercorn Sauce.

❄ Suitable for freezing.

▤ Reheat from frozen.

# LEEKS AND HAM

8 large leeks, trimmed, split and washed
8 thin slices of cooked ham
275 ml (½ pint) Basic White Sauce (page 6)
1 tablespoon Worcestershire Sauce
125 g (4 oz) cheese, grated
50 g (2 oz) breadcrumbs

1 Cook the whole leeks in a large pan of boiling water for 20 minutes. Drain well.
2 Wrap the slices of ham round the leeks and place in a buttered, ovenproof dish.
3 Make the white sauce. Remove from the heat, stir in 50 g (2 oz) of the grated cheese and the Worcestershire Sauce.
4 Pour the sauce over the leeks and ham and sprinkle with the cheese and breadcrumbs.
5 Put into a fairly hot oven at 190°C/375°F/Gas Mark 5 for 20–25 minutes.
6 Serve as a light lunch or supper snack.

**Variation:** replace the Worcestershire Sauce with Lea & Perrins' Spiced Peppercorn Sauce.

❄ Suitable for freezing.

▤ Reheat from frozen.

*Leeks and Ham*
*Wholemeal Tomato Quiche*

# PIZZA

*For the pizza dough:*
225 g (8 oz) plain flour
25 g (1 oz) margarine or butter
1 teaspoon bicarbonate of soda
1 teaspoon cream of tartar
milk, to mix
*For the topping:*
1 onion, peeled and sliced
1 tablespoon oil
397 g (14 oz) can of chopped tomatoes
2 tablespoons Lea & Perrins' Chilli and Garlic Sauce
2 teaspoons tomato purée
125 g (4 oz) cheese, grated
2–3 slices of salami, to garnish

1 To make the dough, sift the dry ingredients together, rub in the margarine or butter and mix to a soft dough with a little milk. Refrigerate.
2 Fry the onion gently in the oil, add the chopped tomatoes in juice, Chilli and Garlic Sauce and tomato purée.
3 Simmer for 5–10 minutes to reduce the liquid. Cool.
4 Form the dough into a round approximately 18 cm (7 inches) in diameter and place on a greased baking sheet.
5 Sprinkle with half the grated cheese, top with the tomato mixture and finally sprinkle over the remainder of the cheese.
6 Slice or quarter the salami to garnish.
7 Bake in a fairly hot oven at 190°C/375°F/Gas Mark 5 for 20–25 minutes, or until the pizza base is cooked and the cheese is bubbling and golden brown.
8 Delicious served either hot or cold, with a salad. Ideal for a party – cook in a square or oblong and cut into fingers.

**Variation:** replace the Chilli and Garlic Sauce with Worcestershire Sauce.

❄ Suitable for freezing.

# HAM AND MUSHROOM STUFFED AUBERGINES

*Serves 4*                                        *200°C/400°F/Gas Mark 6*

2 medium-size aubergines
2 tablespoons oil
1 medium-size onion, finely chopped
1 clove of garlic, crushed
75 g (3 oz) mushrooms, roughly chopped
50 g (2 oz) ham, diced
1 tablespoon chopped parsley
1 tomato, skinned and chopped
50 g (2 oz) fresh breadcrumbs
1 tablespoon Lea and Perrins' Chilli and Garlic Sauce
seasoning, to taste
50 g (2 oz) cheese, grated

1  Cut the aubergines in half lengthways and scoop out the flesh with a metal spoon being careful not to split the skin, and leaving at least a 0.5 cm (¼ inch) shell.
2  Chop the flesh roughly.
3  Heat the oil in a large pan and fry the onion and garlic for 2–3 minutes.
4  Stir in the mushrooms, aubergine flesh, ham, parsley, tomato, breadcrumbs, Chilli and Garlic Sauce and seasoning to taste. Mix well and cook for 2–3 minutes.
5  Place the aubergine shells in a baking dish and fill with the mixture. Sprinkle with the grated cheese.
6  Cover with foil and bake in a hot oven at 200°C/400°F/Gas Mark 6, for 30 minutes, then uncover and cook for a further 5–10 minutes until crisp and golden. Serve immediately.

**Variation:** replace the Chilli and Garlic Sauce with Lea and Perrins' Spiced Peppercorn or Worcestershire Sauce.

❄  Suitable for freezing.

▤  Reheat from frozen.

# Snacks, Savouries and Quick Meals

## Tangy Cheese and Tomato Sandwich Filling

*Makes approximately 4 rounds*

---

8 slices of bread
butter, for spreading
*For the filling:*
50 g (2 oz) butter or margarine, softened
125 g (4 oz) cheese, grated
3 spring onions, chopped
1 tablespoon Worcestershire Sauce
1 tablespoon tomato ketchup

1 To make the filling, soften the butter and gradually add the grated cheese, chopped onions, Worcestershire Sauce and tomato ketchup.
2 Beat well until a spreading consistency is obtained.
3 Spread onto buttered bread, top with another slice, cut diagonally into 4 and serve.

**Variations:** ring the changes with the type of bread used, e.g. white, granary, wholemeal, etc. For a 'low fat' version, use low fat soft cheese or sieved cottage cheese instead of a hard cheese.

# SPICED CHICKEN SANDWICH FILLING

*Makes approximately 8 rounds*

16 slices of bread
butter, for spreading
*For the filling:*
75 g (3 oz) butter or margarine, softened
225 g (8 oz) cooked chicken, finely minced
1½ tablespoons Worcestershire Sauce
shredded lettuce

1 Mix together all the ingredients for the filling, except the lettuce, until you have a fine, spreading paste.
2 Alternatively, use an electric blender or food processor to blend all the ingredients until a spreading consistency is obtained.
3 Spread the filling on buttered bread, add a layer of finely chopped crisp lettuce and top with another slice of buttered bread.
4 Cut diagonally into 4 and serve.

**Variations:** ring the changes with the type of bread used, e.g. white, granary, wholemeal, etc. For an alternative flavour, replace the Worcestershire Sauce with one of the three Culinary Sauces – Chilli and Garlic, Lemon and Herbs, or Spiced Peppercorn. This recipe is also delicious spread as a pâté on hot, buttered toast.

# WORCESTERSHIRE CHEESE STRAWS AND BISCUITS

*Makes approximately 60 straws*
*or 35 biscuits*

*220°C/425°F/Gas Mark 7*

---

225 g (8 oz) plain flour
150 g (5 oz) butter
125 g (4 oz) cheese, finely grated
1 tablespoon Worcestershire Sauce
softened savoury herb butter, to spread (page 14)

1 Sieve the flour and rub in the butter until the mixture resembles fine breadcrumbs; add the cheese.
2 Bind with the Worcestershire Sauce and knead lightly.
3 Roll out gently onto a floured board to about ½ cm (¼ inch) thick.
4 Cut the pastry into very narrow fingers and place them on lightly greased baking trays.
5 Also cut out some pastry 'rings' using two different sized round cutters.
6 Bake in a hot oven at 220°C/425°F/Gas Mark 7 for 8–10 minutes, or until crisp and golden brown.
7 When cool, serve the straws through the rings.
8 The savoury cheese pastry can also be used to make a selection of different shaped biscuits which are baked in exactly the same way.
9 Serve the biscuits with the spicy herb butter, either piped onto the biscuits, or used to sandwich them together.

**Variation:** replace the Worcestershire Sauce with Lea & Perrins' Chilli and Garlic Sauce in both the pastry and the flavoured butter.

❋ Suitable for freezing.

# WORCESTERSHIRE CHEESE AND HAM SCONES

*Makes approximately 18 small scones*     *220°C/425°F/Gas Mark 7*

225 g (8 oz) self-raising flour
1 teaspoon baking powder
1 teaspoon dried mustard
50 g (2 oz) margarine or butter
75 g (3 oz) cheese, grated
75 g (3 oz) cooked ham, diced
2 tablespoons Worcestershire Sauce
approximately 7 tablespoons milk
beaten egg or milk, for glazing

1 Sieve the self-raising flour, baking powder and dried mustard into a bowl.
2 Rub in the 50 g (2 oz) of margarine or butter.
3 Add the grated cheese and diced ham and mix well.
4 Form into a dough with the Worcestershire Sauce and milk. Knead well.
5 Roll out to 1 cm (½ inch) in thickness, cut into rounds and place on a greased baking sheet.
6 Glaze with egg or milk and bake at 220°C/425°F/Gas Mark 7 for 12–15 minutes, or until risen and golden brown.
7 Serve warm or cold, split and buttered.

❄ Suitable for freezing.

▤ Reheat from frozen.

# HAM AND PINEAPPLE TOASTIES

*Serves 2–4*

---

4 thick slices of bread
125 g (4 oz) cream cheese
3 pineapple rings, chopped
2 slices cooked ham, chopped
1 teaspoon chopped chives, plus extra to garnish
1 tablespoon Worcestershire Sauce
50 g (2 oz) grated cheese

1  Toast the bread on one side.
2  Mix together the cream cheese, chopped pineapple, chopped ham, chives and Worcestershire Sauce.
3  Spread the untoasted side of the bread with the cream cheese mixture and sprinkle it evenly with grated cheese.
4  Return to the grill until it is heated through and the cheese is golden brown.
5  Serve immediately, garnished with chopped chives.

*Worcestershire Cheese and Ham Scones*

Worcestershire Cheese Straws and Biscuits

Ham and
Pineapple Toasties

# CHICKEN LIVER PÂTÉ

*Serves 8*

---

50 g (2 oz) butter
1 small onion, chopped
1 clove of garlic, crushed
4 rashers lean bacon, chopped
225 g (8 oz) chicken livers, chopped
a pinch of thyme
1 tablespoon Lea & Perrins' Spiced Peppercorn Sauce
1 tablespoon brandy or sherry
seasoning, to taste

1 Melt the butter in a pan, add the onion, garlic and bacon and fry gently for approximately 2 minutes.
2 Add the chopped livers and the thyme, season and cook gently for about 5 minutes.
3 Add the Spiced Peppercorn Sauce and brandy, mix well and remove from the heat.
4 Put into a blender or food processor and when smooth, transfer into one large or 8 small individual serving dishes.
5 Chill before serving as a starter with toast, or as a snack lunch with crusty bread and salad for 4 people.

❄ Suitable for freezing. Defrost thoroughly before serving.

# MUSHROOM AND WATERCRESS PÂTÉ

*Serves 4*

---

2 tablespoons oil
1 medium-size onion, chopped
2 cloves of garlic, crushed
2 sticks of celery, finely chopped
225 g (8 oz) mushrooms, chopped
1 tablespoon Lea and Perrins' Lemon and Herbs Sauce
1 tablespoon flour
1 bunch of watercress, roughly chopped
3 tablespoons soured cream
seasoning, to taste

1 Heat the oil in a large frying pan and fry the onion, garlic and celery for approximately 5 minutes.
2 Add the mushrooms to the pan and continue cooking.
3 Add the Lemon and Herbs Sauce, mix well and sprinkle in the flour. Cook for one minute, stirring constantly.
4 Remove from the heat and blend or liquidise with the roughly chopped watercress, soured cream and seasoning, until the desired texture is achieved.
5 Spoon into 4 individual ramekin dishes or small pots and chill thoroughly. Serve as a starter or snack with toast, crusty bread or pitta bread. Alternatively, serve as a dip with raw vegetables.

# TUNA SPECIAL

*Serves 6*

---

6 thick slices of bread
198 g (7 oz) can of tuna
50 g (2 oz) mayonnaise
1 tablespoon Worcestershire Sauce
75 g (3 oz) cheese, grated
2 tomatoes, sliced

1 Toast the bread on one side.
2 Drain the tuna well and mix with the mayonnaise and Worcestershire Sauce.
3 Spread the tuna mixture on the untoasted side of the bread.
4 Sprinkle with the grated cheese and garnish with sliced tomato.
5 Put under a pre-heated grill, until the mixture has heated through and the cheese has melted. Serve immediately.

# SPAGHETTI WITH BACON AND CHEESE

*Serves 6*

---

575 g (1¼ lb) spaghetti
2 tablespoons oil
1 small onion, peeled and chopped
1 clove of garlic, crushed
225 g (8 oz) lean bacon, cut into small strips
2 tablespoons Lea & Perrins' Chilli and Garlic Sauce
grated parmesan cheese
seasoning, to taste

1 Cook the spaghetti according to the instructions on the packet.
2 Drain, turn it into a deep, heated serving dish and keep it hot.
3 Meanwhile, heat the oil and fry the onion and garlic until lightly coloured.
4 Add the bacon and fry until lightly browned.
5 Add the Chilli and Garlic Sauce, heat through and when bubbling pour it over the spaghetti; add the cheese and mix, season to taste and serve.

**Variations:** try wholemeal spaghetti or wholemeal pasta shapes. For an alternative flavour replace the Chilli and Garlic Sauce with Worcestershire Sauce.

*Spaghetti with Bacon and Cheese*

# SPANISH OMELETTE

*Serves 2*

oil, for frying
2 tomatoes, skinned and chopped
1 small onion or several spring onions, chopped
½ red pepper, de-seeded and chopped
½ green pepper, de-seeded and chopped
1 stick of celery, chopped
4 mushrooms, sliced
4 eggs, beaten
1 tablespoon Lea and Perrins' Chilli and Garlic Sauce

1 Heat the oil in the pan and stir-fry all the vegetables for 2–3 minutes.
2 Add the beaten eggs and the Chilli and Garlic Sauce.
3 Cook quickly until the egg is set underneath.
4 Place for a few seconds under a hot grill to brown the top.
5 Slide out without folding on to a hot plate and serve at once, as a snack, or with crusty bread and salad for a more substantial meal.

**Variations:** for an alternative flavour replace the Chilli and Garlic Sauce with Worcestershire Sauce or Lea and Perrins' Spiced Peppercorn Sauce. Try using up leftover meat and vegetables in this dish.

# TOASTED CHEESE AND BACON ROLLS

*Serves 4*

4 bread rolls
4 rashers of lean bacon, cut into small pieces
1 bunch of spring onions, chopped
1 egg, beaten
125 g (4 oz) cheese, grated
1 tablespoon Worcestershire Sauce
seasoning, to taste

1 Split the rolls in half.
2 Mix all the other ingredients together thoroughly.
3 Divide the mixture between the eight halves of the rolls and spread evenly, taking care to reach the edges.

4 Place under a hot grill for 1 minute and then reduce the heat and continue cooking for 3–5 minutes until all the ingredients are thoroughly cooked and the mixture is golden brown.
5 Serve immediately, as a quick snack on its own or accompanied by a salad.

**Variation:** replace the Worcestershire Sauce with Lea and Perrins' Spiced Peppercorn or Chilli and Garlic Sauce.

# PACIFIC TUNA PIE

*Serves 4–6*                                    *180°C/350°F/Gas Mark 4*

---

2 × 198 g (7 oz) cans of tuna
125 g (4 oz) frozen peas
3 medium-size tomatoes, peeled and sliced
275 ml (½ pint) Basic White Sauce (page 6)
1 tablespoon Worcestershire Sauce
seasoning, to taste
*For the topping:*
ready-salted crisps, crushed
50 g (2 oz) cheese, grated

1 Drain and flake the tuna and cook the peas.
2 Make the white sauce and add the Worcestershire Sauce.
3 Layer half the tuna, white sauce, peas and tomatoes in an ovenproof dish and then repeat the layers with the remaining ingredients, finishing with a layer of crushed crisps and grated cheese.
4 Put into a preheated oven at 180°C/350°F/Gas Mark 4, for 30 minutes. Serve immediately.

# FRENCH ONION SOUP

*Serves 4–6*

butter and oil, for frying
700 g (1½ lb) spanish onions, peeled and sliced into rings
1 tablespoon flour
575 ml (1 pint) well-flavoured stock
1 tablespoon Worcestershire Sauce
4–6 slices of french bread, buttered
4–6 slices of Cheddar cheese
black pepper

1 Heat the butter and oil and fry the onions until golden brown.
2 Stir in the flour and cook gently for 2 minutes.
3 Gradually stir in the stock and Worcestershire Sauce.
4 Bring to the boil and then simmer for 25 minutes.
5 Pour into warmed bowls, float a slice of bread with a slice of cheese on in each bowl, sprinkle with black pepper and place under a preheated grill, just to melt the cheese. Serve immediately.

*French Onion Soup*

# MUSHROOM SOUP

*Serves 4*

---

25 g (1 oz) butter or margarine
25 g (1 oz) flour
275 ml (½ pint) chicken stock
275 ml (½ pint) milk
125 g (4 oz) mushrooms, sliced
1 tablespoon Worcestershire Sauce
1 tablespoon lemon juice
2 tablespoons natural low-fat yogurt
1 tablespoon chopped parsley

1 Place all the ingredients except the lemon juice, parsley and low-fat yogurt in a large saucepan.
2 Bring to the boil, whisking continuously, over a moderate heat.
3 Cover and simmer for 10 minutes.
4 Remove from the heat and stir in the lemon juice.
5 Pour into a warmed serving dish or tureen. Garnish with a swirl of yogurt and chopped parsley.
6 Serve with toast or crusty bread.

**Variations:** use skimmed milk for a low-fat version. For an alternative flavour replace the Worcestershire Sauce with Lea & Perrins' Lemon and Herbs Sauce (omit the fresh lemon juice).

# SPICY TOMATO CHOWDER

*Serves 4–6*

---

300 g (10½ oz) can of condensed tomato soup (undiluted)
425 ml (¾ pint) milk
397 g (14 oz) can of tomatoes, sieved
340 g (12 oz) can of sweetcorn, drained
2 tablespoons Worcestershire Sauce
1 teaspoon sugar
seasoning, to taste
50 g (2 oz) cheese, grated

1 Combine all the ingredients, except the cheese, with seasoning to taste in a large saucepan. Bring to the boil, stirring constantly.
2 Simmer gently for 5 minutes and pour into a hot serving bowl or individual bowls.
3 Sprinkle the grated cheese on top.
4 Put the bowl or bowls under a preheated grill until the cheese melts and is bubbling. Serve immediately, with crusty bread.

# MICROWAVE HINTS AND TIPS

As a microwave-owner you will know that experimentation is all important. Here we offer some hints and tips to help you increase your range of quick and easy recipes.

Use your microwave oven handbook as a guide to times, power levels, dish types and special techniques.

*Chicken drumsticks brushed with*
*Worcestershire Sauce, Chilli and*
*Garlic Sauce, Spiced Peppercorn Sauce*

Baked potatoes with prawn topping and cheese and spring onion topping

Pork chops in Barbecue Sauce

**Browning sauces**
For chicken, chops, beefburgers and kebabs, simply brush Worcester-shire Sauce, Spiced Peppercorn Sauce or Chilli and Garlic Sauce over the meat before cooking.

See 'Sauces, Marinades and Dressings' (page 6). Use these marinades and sauces to add colour and interest to meat and poultry.

**Baked potatoes and toppings**
Baked potatoes make a healthy meal and are very quick and easy in a microwave. Use the following ideas to turn them into interesting quick snacks.

When cooked, cut the potatoes in half, remove the centres, mix well with Worcestershire Sauce or a Culinary Sauce and a combination of prawns, tuna, cooked meats, or cheese with chopped spring onions, chives, parsley, etc. Fill the potato shells with your chosen stuffing and reheat in the microwave oven.

Try the recipe for Baked Potatoes with Cheese and Bacon (page 61).

Top the halved, baked potatoes with Pizza topping (page 74).

Flavour baked beans with a Lea & Perrins' sauce, spoon on to a halved, baked potato and reheat.

Make a topping of sliced tomato, grated cheese and a sprinkling of the Lea & Perrins' sauce of your choice and reheat.

Flavour canned minced beef with a Lea & Perrins' sauce, spoon on to a halved, baked potato and reheat.

Try the recipes for Mushroom Sauce, Tomato Sauce and Savoury Butters in the chapter on 'Sauces, Marinades and Dressings' (page 6).

**Toast or split muffins**
Add the Lea & Perrins' sauce of your choice to baked beans, scrambled eggs or grated cheese and serve hot from the microwave on toast or muffins.

Try Tuna Special (page 83) or Ham and Pineapple Toasties (page 80) as toppings on toast or muffins. Pizza topping (page 74) can be added to split muffins or french bread to make quick mini-pizzas.

**Poaching fish**
Arrange the fish in a suitable container, sprinkle with Lea & Perrins' Lemon and Herbs Sauce, cover and cook in the microwave.

**Soups and casseroles**
Add variety to soups and casseroles cooked in your microwave with the addition of a Lea & Perrins' sauce. Always add the sauce before cooking and add salt, if required, after cooking.

**Meat**
Cuts which require slower cooking benefit from being marinated for 2–3 hours prior to cooking, using any of the marinade recipes in the chapter on 'Sauces, Marinades and Dressings' (page 6).

# INDEX

Aubergines:
  Ham and mushroom
    stuffed aubergines  75
  Moussaka  31
Bacon:
  Baked potatoes with
    cheese and bacon  61
  Cauliflower and bacon
    savoury  62
  Spaghetti with bacon
    and cheese  84
  Toasted cheese and
    bacon rolls  86
Baked potatoes,
  microwave  94
Baked potatoes with cheese
  and bacon  61
Barbecue sauce  8
Barbecued chicken
  wings  56
Basic white sauce  6
Beef carbonade  30
Beef, minced:
  Chilli con carne  36
  Meatballs with peppers
    and tomatoes  34
  Moussaka  31
  Spicy layer cottage
    pie  38
Beef provençale  35
Beefburgers:
  Barbecued  56
  Beefburgers with orange
    barbecued sauce  39
  Sauces for  8, 10
Biscuits, Worcestershire
  cheese straws and  78
Browning sauces,
  microwave  94
Butters, savoury  14

Cabbage au gratin  60
Cauliflower and bacon
  savoury  62
Cheese:
  Baked potatoes with
    cheese and bacon  61
  Cabbage au gratin  60
  Spaghetti with bacon
    and cheese  84
  Tangy cheese and
    tomato sandwich
    filling  76

Toasted cheese and
  bacon rolls  86
Worcestershire cheese
  and ham scones  79
Worcestershire cheese
  straws and
  biscuits  78
Chicken:
  Barbecued chicken
    wings  56
  Chicken and mushroom
    vol-au-vents  51
  Chicken croquettes  59
  Chicken liver pâté  82
  Chicken mornay  48
  Chicken, pineapple and
    pasta  55
  Chicken provençale  54
  Chicken with
    peaches  50
  Paprika chicken  58
  Spiced chicken sandwich
    filling  77
  Stir-fried hot spiced
    chicken with
    peppers  52
Chilli con carne  36
Chilli marinade, hot  11
Chinese braised
  vegetables  68
Cod in caper sauce  19
Cod provençale  15
Conversion tables  5
Cottage pie, spicy
  layer  38
Courgettes:
  Courgettes
    provençale  64
  Lamb in courgettes and
    tomatoes  44
Crunchy savoury
  pancakes  67
Dips and savoury
  butters  14
Dressings  12
Dutch beef stew  37

Fish  15-29
Fish cakes, lemon and
  herb  21
Fish meunière  16
Fish, microwave  94
Flaky fish plait  20

Flans:
  Prawn and egg flan  22
  Smoked haddock and
    tomato flan  23
  Sweetcorn and ham
    flan  66
  Wholemeal tomato
    quiche  71
Flavoured mayonnaise
  dressings  12
Foil wrapped lamb  43
French onion soup  88
Ham:
  Crunchy savoury
    pancakes  67
  Ham and mushroom
    stuffed aubergines  75
  Ham and pineapple
    toasties  80
  Leeks and ham  72
  Sweetcorn and ham
    flan  66
  Worcestershire cheese
    and ham scones  79
Honey and pineapple
  marinade  11
Hot chilli marinade  11

Kebabs:
  Pork kebabs  42
  Sauces and marinades
    for  8, 11
Kidneys, spicy braised  46

Lamb:
  Foil wrapped lamb  43
  Lamb in courgettes and
    tomatoes  44
Lamb chops
  Barbecued  56
  Sauces and marinades
    for  8, 11
Leeks and ham  72
Lemon and herb fish
  cakes  21

Marinades  10-11
Mayonnaise dressings  12
Meat and poultry  30-59
Meatballs with peppers and
  tomatoes  34
Microwave hints and
  tips  92-4

Moussaka   31
Mushrooms:
   Mushroom and
      watercress pâté   82
   Mushroom sauce   7
   Mushroom soup   90
   Prawn, mushroom and
      lemon pancakes   18

Oil and vinegar
   dressing   12
Omelette, Spanish   86
Onion soup, French   88

Pacific tuna pie   87
Pancakes:
   Crunchy savoury
      pancakes   67
   Prawn, mushroom and
      lemon pancakes   18
Paprika chicken   58
Pasta dishes:
   Chicken, pineapple and
      pasta   55
   Spaghetti with bacon
      and cheese   84
Pâtés:
   Chicken liver pâté   82
   Mushroom and
      watercress pâté   82
   Sardine and lemon
      pâté   24
Peppers, stuffed green   63
Pizza   74
Pork chops: see also lamb
      chops
   Pork chops in orange
      sauce   42
Pork fillet, stir-fried   52
Pork kebabs   42
Pork spare ribs, sweet and
      sour   40
Potatoes:
   Baked potatoes with
      cheese and bacon   61
   Microwave baked
      potatoes   94
   Potato salad special   66
Prawns:
   Prawn and egg flan   22
   Prawn, mushroom and
      lemon pancakes   18

Quiche: see Flans
Quick meals   76–91

Rice, Spanish   70

Salads:
   Dressings   12
   Potato salad special   66
   Salad niçoise   28
   Salmon and sweetcorn
      salad   26
   Tuna salad   27
Salmon and sweetcorn
      salad   26
Sandwich fillings:
   Ham and pineapple   80
   Spiced chicken   77
   Tangy cheese and
      tomato   76
Sardine and lemon
      pâté   24
Sauces, marinades and
      dressings   6–14
Sauces:
   Barbecue sauce   8
   Basic white sauce   6
   Caper sauce, cod in   19
   Mushroom sauce   7
   Orange barbecued sauce,
      beefburgers with   39
   Orange sauce, pork chops
      in   42
   Spicy tomato sauce   10
Sausages, sauces and
      marinades for   8, 11
Savoury butters   14
Scones, Worcestershire
      cheese and ham   79
Smoked haddock and
      tomato flan   23
Snacks, savouries and quick
      meals   76–91
Soups:
   French onion soup   88
   Mushroom soup   90
   Spicy tomato
      chowder   91
Spaghetti with bacon and
      cheese   84
Spanish omelette   86
Spanish rice   70
Spiced chicken sandwich
      filling   77
Spicy braised kidneys   46
Spicy layer cottage pie   38
Spicy tomato chowder   91
Spicy tomato sauce   10

Steak:
   Beef carbonade   30
   Beef provençale   35
   Dutch beef stew   37
   Stir-fried hot spiced
      chicken with
      peppers   52
   Stuffed green peppers   63
   Sweet and sour pork spare
      ribs   40
Sweetcorn:
   Salmon and sweetcorn
      salad   26
   Sweetcorn and ham
      flan   66

Tangy cheese and tomato
      sandwich filling   76
Toasted sandwiches:
   Ham and pineapple
      toasties   80
   Toasted cheese and
      bacon rolls   86
   Tuna special   83
Tomatoes:
   Lamb in courgettes and
      tomatoes   44
   Smoked haddock and
      tomato flan   23
   Spicy tomato
      chowder   91
   Spicy tomato sauce   10
   Tomato marinade   11
Tuna fish:
   Pacific tuna pie   87
   Salad niçoise   28
   Tuna salad   27
   Tuna special   83

Vegetable dishes   60–75

Watercress pâté,
      mushroom and   82
White sauce, basic   6
Wholemeal tomato
      quiche   71
Worcestershire cheese and
      ham scones   79
Worcestershire cheese
      straws and
      biscuits   78